In the name of God, the Most Beneficent, the Most Merciful. All praise is to God, the Lord of the worlds. I invoke His aid throughout my journey, and I ask that He showers us all in His endless love, His all-encompassing Mercy, and His wholesome guidance. I am nothing without His support.

HOLDING
SPACE
for the
SUN

JAMAL CADOURA

**THOUGHT
CATALOG**
Books

THOUGHTCATALOG.COM
NEW YORK · LOS ANGELES

THOUGHT CATALOG Books

Copyright © 2022 Jamal Cadoura. All rights reserved.

Published by Thought Catalog Books, an imprint of the digital magazine Thought Catalog, which is owned and operated by The Thought & Expression Company LLC, an independent media organization based in Brooklyn, New York and Los Angeles, California.

This book was produced by Chris Lavergne and Noelle Beams with art direction and design by KJ Parish. Special thanks to Bianca Sparacino for creative editorial direction and Isidoros Karamitopoulos for circulation management.

Visit us at *thoughtcatalog.com* and *shopcatalog.com*.

Made in the United States of America.

ISBN 978-1-949759-48-8

But perhaps you hate a thing and it is good for you; and perhaps you love a thing and it is bad for you. And Allah knows, while you know not.

The Holy Quran, 2:216

To you, my love. Thank you for being my beacon of hope during my darkest days. For loving me, even as I struggled to push myself forward. For seeing the greatness in me, even as I spiraled downward. I am indebted to you for your unending support, your warm encouragement, your soft words, and your effervescent spirit. My life would be devoid of purpose without your smile and your essence. I am grateful to be yours. Every struggle I endured has led me to you. And that's what makes it all worth it. I love you, Hanan Chami.

Life is a beautiful journey filled with highs, lows, peaks, and valleys. And oftentimes, we lose our way. We stumble, we fall, we experience insufferable defeats and palpable grief. But we rise, we rebuild, and we serve as radiant lights for those lost along their paths. I'm still uncovering so many elements of myself. Pieces awaiting my watchful eyes, my mending heart, and my eager soul. I do not possess the answers. But each day, I awake with a renewed hope. A chance to change. An opportunity to bid my old self goodbye, to collect the debris, and to rebuild a future teeming with promise, potential, and the love I hope to honor this world with.

And believe me, if it is meant for you, it will find you again.

I often found myself recounting past loves and past opportunities. Yearning for them to return. For them to suddenly realize my vibrant heart and its vast intricacies. To burst through every barrier and to claim, and cherish, the inner light I house.

But oftentimes, I would be left reeling. Wondering why I was never good enough to be reclaimed. Why no one would fight for me the way I fought for them. I was chasing unavailability, hoping that it would patch the holes in my heart. That it would finally bequeath meaning to my existence.

Yet the more I chased, the further I became from myself. From my own inner warmth and vibrancy that made life meaningful. And that is when I ceased the chasing, the settling, and the hoping for others to return. I reclaimed myself, refusing to sail in ships that were headed toward the islands of unrequited love and heartache. The islands that I had no business visiting.

And you don't need to tolerate less than you deserve, either. Because if you truly believe that you're worthy of more, you wouldn't settle for anyone's half-hearted attempts and hurtful inabilities. You would honor your heart and place it into hands strong enough to hold you; into souls loving enough to reciprocate; and into spaces that honor your worth, a luxurious museum housing the finest relics.

Because what is destined for you will find you. Even if you hide. Even if you traverse the roughest terrains. The harshest deserts. The most unrelenting seas and barren plains. And it will find you when you are emitting authenticity. Smiling as you're living in your truths and standing firm on the borders of your heart.

You won't need to be anything more or anything less. You will simply be yourself. And that is when you will reap what you're worthy of. That is when you will know that everything played out in your favor, and your plans were always meant for something more.

Somehow, you've always
made it through.

And this time, it'll
be the same. You'll
heal, you'll grow, and
you'll smile again.

You'll have moments where you want to quit. Moments where tears stream down your face, where your heart breaks repeatedly, and where you struggle to remember your worth and your purpose. You feel that you're too far gone to be rescued. That you're going to drown beneath your sorrows as the world carries on and buries the legacy you were determined to build.

But life is never as bleak as your mind deceives you into believing. You've had similar moments. Times where you swore you would never move on, where you would never love again, and where the sun wouldn't rise upon you.

Yet you picked up the jagged pieces of your heart, dusted your shoulders off, and moved on. You refused to give up. To believe that it was your end.

And this time, it is the same. No matter how broken you feel, or how defeated you are, you can always start again. You can always take your ashes, plant them in the ground, and allow a new you to grow.

You are only temporarily halted. Never permanently defeated. Never down for the entirety of your life. Just as you have overcome prior difficulties and evolved beautifully, you will do the same now. You will show the resilience of your heart and the value of your soul. You will move on toward greatness and claim everything you've always been worthy of.

Yes, you overthink.

But it's because you care.
You never want to look
back and wish that you did
more. You give your all,
and you love in ways that
others can only imagine.

And that's what makes
your heart special.

Before, I'd shame myself for being too open. Fault my heart for loving too deeply and pouring its precious love into spaces that were far too jagged and rigid to hold it. Curse the skies for making me so emotional, where love isn't just a word, but an ocean that covers my entirety; where effort isn't just a morning text, but a creed that dominates my actions; where pain isn't a few tears, but the unraveling of my soul and the unbecoming of my existence.

I'd give, only to be left stranded, watching the dust of their departure cloud my body. I faded into oblivion countless times. I grew so exasperated. And I tried changing my love. Tried turning a universe into a tiny speck.

But it never worked. I always found myself brimming with love. With flowers emerging from my mouth. With light cascading down my heart. With sweetness jumping off my lips.

And eventually, I stopped trying to change. I surrendered to my loving ways. I realized that my love wasn't the issue, but who I was choosing to grant it to was. I didn't need to change something beautiful. We never ruin a grand portrait. We only change its position. I didn't need to ruin, or change, what God planted in my being. Nor did I need to allow coldness to harden my heart.

I needed to honor my worth and to maximize my inner gifts. And now, I realize that my love, and my emotionality, aren't a curse, but a blessing. I am able to feel things so deeply. To fully immerse myself in life's joys and wonders, while others may deprive themselves of such bounties.

I am proud that I care. Proud that I refuse to put up facades of heartlessness. That I do not wear a mask of falsehood or put a curtain of darkness around my soul. I want to share my inner intricacies with the world. I do not wish to be like others. I want to know that I left no stone unturned, and that if I do walk away, I can hold my head high without wishing I could have done more.

I am honored to be able to experience love in its entirety, whereas others experience unsatisfactory fractions. I am honored to not only change myself with my heart, but to also change others, and to watch as the world transforms within love's fingertips. I am content with my heart breaking, because I know it will always rebuild into something greater. Something so powerful and luminous that I wouldn't have it any other way.

Sometimes, the people you love won't stay. And that's ok. They weren't meant to. Their purpose was to show you the depths of your heart, and to teach you how to honor your worth.

I would fixate on the people who left. Watch their footprints imprint the tattered, dusted rug of my heart. Hear their final goodbyes ringing in my ears. Replay all the glorified scenes we shared. I had such a hard time letting go. Detaching from temporary moments that I believed were my forever.

I wanted to hang on. I'd clutch the keys to the gates of my soul so tightly. Believing that maybe they'd come back if I made it too hard to go. I hated goodbyes so much that I was willing to rip my insides instead.

I'd constantly shame myself. I couldn't believe I was worthy. Because if I had any intrinsic value, I wouldn't be left heartbroken and abandoned. Someone would finally stay and fight for me, the same way I stayed and fought for others. I was never afraid to pour everything I had into every opportunity. To watch pieces of myself go down the drain, with uncertainty swirling my mind. My heart broke countless times and I forfeited so many battles in love's war.

And though I never reclaimed what I lost, I gained a newfound perspective. I learned that my worth is not in the hands of others, but in the way I show up. In the wholesome love I shower others in. The honest ways I express myself. The loyalty I brandish, even when darkness is on the horizon and someone is going under.

And that's the beauty of a goodbye: it removes those who aren't meant for you and fills the newly emptied space with self-love and a mirror reflecting the worth you've had all along. You would never be able to see the beauty within your heart, if its high walls weren't broken so light could seep through and the goodness could shine brightly. You would never realize just how honorably you show up and how far you're willing to go.

Departures once broke me. But now, I am indebted to them. For they have shown me sides of myself I would never have been known. Sides that I am proud of. I see my strength, my honor, and my worth all staring back at me.

And now, I no longer mourn farewells. I embrace the impending lessons. I honor myself for remaining loyal to love and goodness. That's all I know, and there is never any other way for me to be. And without heartbreak, I'd never have seen what I truly possess.

Walk away. Even if it hurts. Even if your heart breaks. Because you deserve to be happy, and you can't stay where your heart doesn't belong.

Leaving hurts. But tolerating less than you deserve hurts more. Because what you choose, and commit to, is a reflection of what you think about yourself and your worth.

If you decide to tolerate mediocrity, subpar efforts, and coldness, it is because you do not believe you deserve better. You believe that your voice is unequal to the voice of another, and that your needs shouldn't be placed above theirs.

Still, your hurt offers you an opportunity to see the way you view yourself, and which parts still require your attention, your care, and your love. You can walk away, not only to reclaim yourself, but to start healing your wounds and learning to say no.

Because the longer you tolerate what you don't deserve, the more your wounds will grow, and the more you will place your needs on the backburner. It's time to let go of the trauma bonds. The relationships and the people who feed your old patterns of chasing love and attention to fill your inner voids. You're worthy of so much more.

And it starts with bidding farewell to the old, so that you may create the new. You walk away, not only to send them a message, but to also push yourself toward change and improvement.

Yes, it hurts. But heartache doesn't necessitate avoidance. The pain you feel today, will be the gratitude that fills your heart tomorrow, as you're in the right relationship, the right spaces, and the right environments that nurture your heart and facilitate your growth.

Don't be afraid to
express yourself.
Your true thoughts will
never ruin a genuine
connection. And if
someone leaves after
you express them, they
were never meant for
you to begin with.

Many of us fear expressing ourselves. We believe that if we open our hearts and show our fullest depths, we will be abandoned. We fear that others won't see our vibrant love and openness, but instead our shortcomings and our deficiencies. The broken, fractured pieces of ourselves that we hide, along with all the flaws inscribed upon them.

We fear that our words will be the soldiers that push another beyond the bounds of their patience. That our needs, our thoughts, and our desires will be too overwhelming. So we put on our fake smiles, don our costumes, and pretend to be someone we're not. We desire their acceptance so badly, that we fall short in giving them something real to bond with.

And this is why we fail to connect authentically. People are either in love with a façade, or we're not feeling safe, welcomed, and accepted in the union. The relationship was built upon sticks and straws. A faulty foundation that was never meant to weather real storms.

That's why we must honor ourselves. We must show who we are, so that we can determine who's meant for us, and who we can peacefully let go of. Vulnerability is a strength. It gives people a chance to see us in our rawest, purest forms. It gives them a home that they can settle in.

And whoever leaves is merely creating space for those who will love us in our entirety. The very way that we deserve to be loved. We can't settle for less. We've always been meant for more, and it's time that we honor it by refusing to stay in spaces that cannot honor who we are. Spaces that require us to be everything other than the shining gems we are.

You may never love anyone the same. And that's ok. You're not supposed to. As you grow, your love will change, and it'll require you to find someone who can appreciate it and return what you deserve.

The hardest part about change is embracing uncertainty. Having to take the debris of your heart from beneath the ash of your unbecoming and build something new. You struggle to take a step forward, because the past has its claws in your back. Taunting you. Replaying your heartbreak. Telling you that you'll never love anyone the same way.

But you shouldn't. You are not mere ink on a paper, change-less and dull. You are an irreplaceable portrait, constantly absorbing new colors and new designs. An endless work of art. A vast city that will never be found the same as it was left.

You won't be able to love anyone the same, because you're going to grow. Through the heartache, the pain, the suf-fering. You're going to take your ashes and turn them into gold. You're going to plant the lessons deeply in your heart and watch as wisdom blooms in the form of firmer bound-aries around your heart, clarity in your mind, and words that vocalize what you want and what you deserve.

There is no way to confine your love. Not being able to love someone the same isn't a detriment. It is a sign of your growth. Because your love changes as you change. And your heart will not be able to love and feel the same once you shed your old layers. It will be different.

You will love, experience, and evolve in unprecedented ways. And then you will find someone who can fit your new mold. Someone who will love you in the ways you've always deserved to be loved.

You don't need closure
from them. Their behavior
is enough. Give yourself
closure by knowing your
worth, walking away,
and honoring what
your heart deserves.

I missed out on golden opportunities to heal. To examine my heart, its vast intricacies, and all of its wounds awaiting my love, my compassion, and my tender hands to stitch them shut.

I thought that I couldn't move on without closure. Without another's permission to set me free from the chains of regret and ineptitude. I needed their words to come and validate me. To gently massage my pain away and lead me toward a new path.

I refused to let go without knowing why another couldn't, or wouldn't, choose me. Without knowing what I could do better. How I could finally show them my worth, my qualities, and my value, so that they would magically realize what they were missing out on and stay. To prove to me that I was worthy, and that I was something more than just a page in their mental yearbook. An insignificant time-stamp they'd vaguely recall as another lover would trace their hands along their past.

But slowly, I realized that closure didn't come from anyone else. Closure comes from within. From the realization of my own worth, and from the power of my choice to walk away, and to let go of anything, and anyone, that does not want to be held onto. My grip is too precious to cling to disintegrating cliffs. Staying somewhere unfit for me merely lowers my worth.

And you are the same. You don't need anyone's permission to move on. True closure is realizing your worth, letting go, and loving your heart enough to grant it people, places, and experiences that fill it with mutual respect, love, and care. Their words will never set you free. But your self-love will. And it's time that you disregard their closure and look ahead to brighter days. To days that are so eager and hopeful, that they're cheering you on and begging you to come sooner.

Each day, you'll feel a little better, and you'll let go a little more. Be patient, and give your heart a chance to heal.

Not every day will be easy. Some days, you'll feel off. Reeling for answers and for a renewed purpose. You'll spend hours raking your mind and hoping that some wisdom will magically sprout to resolve all of your wounds and your ailments.

On other days, you will be riddled with pain and with agony. Reminiscing on everything you've lost. On the people, the places, and the memories that have passed you by. You become a prisoner in a worn cell, staring out of the bars and mourning how everyone is progressing and forgetting you. Letting you recede into the background to become another memory, another vaguely remembered name.

But eventually, you will recover. Slowly, the light will enter you and it will shine upon all of your goodness. The very qualities that have shown your worth and revealed your profound strength. You've gone through storms and tragedies. Yet you still rise to heal and to claim more.

Because deep down, you know this isn't your end. You've been here before. Down. Defeated. Flailing and yearning for a miracle, as you struggle to hang on and to believe. And yet somehow, you've always found a way to fight back. To regain position at the top and to smile at everything that tried to break you.

You made the right decision in walking away. And it's ok if it hurts. You're allowed to grieve. But remember to be proud of yourself for honoring your worth, and knowing when to let go.

Letting go is never easy. You will lose pieces of yourself. Your tears will fall and your heart will shatter. Your mind will replay all your unsaid words, your absent actions, and everything that you're losing. The future becomes a distant haze, and it's hard to believe that life will go on. That as the sun rises, you can, too. You're allowed to grieve and to mourn the loss. It is your right to not only miss someone, but to also miss the pieces of yourself that they're taking with them.

But it's important to remember that goodbyes entail more than sadness. They also entail hope, because you are realizing your worth, and honoring what you deserve. You're refusing to stay with someone who cannot value you, and your precious soul, in the way it deserves. They entail strength. The ability to overcome your fears, and to head toward another direction where you are a priority, and you're no longer withering away in the background. Tragedies birth realizations, and there is no realization greater than you seeing your worth, and rejecting anything that's less.

Every end is a new beginning. A chance for you to change, to grow, and to forge the life, and the love, you desire. You can lament your losses. You can be angry and disenchanted with life's uncertainties. But you mustn't lose sight of your future. Of the opportunities that you are being invited to embrace, that will honor your worth, your value, and your inner beauty.

Don't be sad that you let go. Be proud of yourself for your strength, your resilience, and your desire for more. You were always meant for more than their broken promises, their unsaid words, and their neglect. And now, you'll attain a better love. An experience so enchanting, that it will quietly tuck your sorrows away, as it paves a new road for you to enjoy.

You always manage to love hard, no matter how broken you're feeling. That's why you're a gift. That's why the world needs you.

So many people pride themselves on callousness and coldness. They are proud of the fact that they've erected impenetrable barriers around their hearts, and that they refuse entry to anyone who knocks. That they'd rather engage in meaningless, fleeting flings, over a wholesome, genuine connection. A bond that engenders kindness, tranquility, and love between two souls.

They've allowed heartbreak to embitter them. They believe that it wasn't another that hurt them, but love. Therefore, they'll never open up again. And if anyone attempts to love them, they will subject them to harsh obstacle courses and a strict, unrelenting checklist. They will force so many people out, and then believe that love is unattainable. But really, it is their own misapprehensions formed from pain.

Heartbreak can harden us. Force us to recoil and to isolate ourselves. It's tiring to seek love, but to only meet heartache and despair. It'll leave many permanently broken, defeated, and despairing.

But not you. You have chosen to maintain your inner openness, and to keep your heart welcoming. You see that love is not the pain imposed upon us from hurt people, but the radiance we all seek that makes sense of our purpose and our suffering. The water that allows barren lands within others to bloom and to prosper with roses and forests of change. You refuse to break completely, even as harsh words, excruciating goodbyes, and a colder society bash against you.

You show so many that you won't be anything other than you, and you will keep your heart soft. That being able to love—especially in today's society—is not a weakness. It is a strength, and it is the very salvation that guides so many people back to their greater purpose. You won't be molded by pain or society's false beliefs. You will uphold your values and ensure that the world blossoms under your purity.

And that's why you're a gift. You stay true to who you are, to your loving ways and your kindness. You refuse to follow the heartbroken and embittered. You walk your own path and express love in needed ways. And it is your love that aids the world's healing, that inspires others to tear down their barriers so that they may form new connections. Without it, we would never be able to move on.

You might be struggling
to let them go, but
that doesn't mean that
they're meant for you.
Because some people
enter your life only to
teach you how to fight
for yourself and to honor
what you truly deserve.

Pain has a strange way of making you doubt yourself. Pushing you back to people and places that you've long outgrown. It's easier to stay attached to someone, or something, than it is to walk away, to say goodbye, and to welcome change.

You'll often believe, falsely, that you're supposed to stay with someone just because it hurts too much to leave. To say enough and to finally venture elsewhere. But pain doesn't necessitate your commitment. Pain often symbolizes your growth, and your departure from your outmoded, unhealthy ways.

You should be with someone because you want to. Because they add value to your life, and you add value to theirs. The both of you share a genuine bond that facilitates greater love, growth, and companionship. There's an authentic, mutual enjoyment, and you both desire the same elements in a relationship.

Still, it hurts to bid farewell. You'll reminisce on the good times, and your mind will deceive you into thinking that there isn't anyone "better." But there is. There is always better than subpar effort, hurtful comments, and unrequited love. But you'll never experience it, if you keep yourself lingering in spaces where you're desperate for others to choose you.

Every experience is a lesson that takes you closer to yourself and to what you deserve. Your heart may be broken, and you may be struggling to believe in a bright future, but these lessons are granting you the wisdom you need to build a better future.

Life changes. You lose love. You lose friends. You lose pieces of yourself that you never imagined would be gone. And then, without you even realizing it, these pieces come back. New love enters. Better friends come along. And a stronger, wiser you is staring back in the mirror. No matter how bad it gets, better days are always waiting, hoping you'll make it there to accept the smiles and the joy that they're offering.

Sometimes, you'll feel broken. Defeated. Lost. You'll feel the aches in your heart and tears will stream down your cheeks as you wonder when the pain will cease. You'll yearn for the older days. When a smile was plastered across your face. When your feet galloped toward new goals and new days with excitement. When the soft hands of an old lover fit warmly into yours. When life was simpler, and you didn't have all these questions circling your mind.

You'll struggle to believe that it can get better. You'll spend time comparing your current life to your old one. You'll miss certain smiling faces. Old relationships. And all the moments that filled your soul with purpose. It will leave gaping holes within your heart, where your love, your hope, and your joy will trickle out.

And you'll wonder if you'll ever smile, love, and regain your footing again. If you'll be able to heal the petals of your heart and to allow new light to enter. Your tears will fall and your heart will shatter repeatedly as you yearn to be renewed.

And someday you will be. You will love again. You will heal your heart. You will reopen your soul as new light enters and new flowers bloom inside. But you must first endure these trials and tribulations. Life necessitates pain, as you bid farewell to your fondest memories. Change is never easy.

Yet it's necessary. It's the only way to create space for new love, new connections, and new opportunities, and to clear out all of the old. The pieces and the people that no longer fit, or that can no longer accompany you on your new journey toward depth and true fulfillment. So don't get lost in your pain. Rejoice in new beginnings; they're your chance to attain everything you're seeking.

Soon, a smiling you will appear in the mirror. New friends will be beside you, showering you in love, light, and support. Accompanying you to new heights of unprecedented growth, where your confidence soars beyond the words of everyone who degraded you; where your luminous smile expels the darkness you've long battled. A new lover will be on the horizon, beckoning you and your tender heart to embrace what they're offering. They will trace their hands across every ounce of your delicate insides, marveling at the sweetness and uniqueness they've always desired. And new opportunities will greet you, acknowledging that you've finally become who you always needed to be to fulfill these deeper, lasting purposes.

And you'll owe it to your strength guiding you toward change. Not only did it create the space for newness, but it also bestowed wisdom upon you through these experiences. So don't give up. Don't lose hope. You are closer than you think, and you'll be so happy that you held on to see it all.

Some days, you'll feel like
you're going backwards.
Like all the progress
you've made was an
illusion. And you'll want
to quit. But you shouldn't.
Healing is never linear,
and it's going to take time.

I have days where I am on top of the world. Where the sunshine is intoxicating and my hope is unbreakable. I am eager to tackle my greatest challenges. My fears are a dissolving mist I drive right through. My heart is renewed, and my worries and concerns are nonexistent. I smile, I laugh loudly, and I invest heavily into my dreams.

Then there are other days. Where my smile is a fleeting image I can't capture. Where my worries and my fears are so overbearing that my chest is tight and my throat closes. My eyes water with perpetual stress. Where I feel hopeless, lost in a maze of life's cruel jokes and despair. Where I wonder if I'm actually healing, and if my struggles will ever become a quiet part of my past. An old page I recollect whenever someone asks for details, but that I rarely reflect on as I peruse other more uplifting, hopeful parts of my life's book.

It's hard to believe in change when I feel that I'm always being pushed back. That I'm constantly battling, and traversing through, the same foreboding terrain. I feel like a prisoner in my own mind. Condemned to suffer a life of endless struggles and crippling chaos.

But I still rise. I refuse to quit. To surrender to the same cycles of generational trauma. To imprison myself in the small dreams and traumas that many others have. I want better for myself. For my future wife and children. I want to show the world that healing does come—even if it's a long process entailing many tears and much heartache.

I remind myself that bad days do not define me. They are merely another component in the intricate body of healing. And they do not mean that I am going backwards nor that I will never achieve my goals. It is these moments that show me the vastness of my soul; the wondrous depths of my mind. I can't expect to quickly dispel my worries and my old attachments. My heart is too loving for that. My soul is too kind and too soft.

The bad days reflect my humanity. The constant struggle that pushes me toward growth and a stronger character, and that serves as little milestones I marvel at as I approach new boundaries. I am only regressing if I'm quitting and abandoning the journey altogether. If I'm refusing to pick up the pen and to write a better chapter. If I'm sulking in misery and believing that I'm meant for the sorrows that others confine themselves to.

I'm learning that healing is volatile. But I don't need to be. Rough moments do not negate my progress, nor do they mean that I'm doomed. I can continue to learn, to grow, and to prosper. Healing takes me all over the place. From the highest mountaintops, to the lowest depths of the most tempestuous seas. Yet I no longer fight. I surrender. I take it all as it comes, and I remind myself that there is no perfect way. There is only growth in small steps and varying stages, and I will make it through.

What hurts now won't hurt forever. Be patient, and trust in your journey. It'll all be worth it when you're smiling, and when your tears have watered the deepest depths of your soul, so that the true you may bloom and prosper.

When you're hurting, it's easy to be negative. To fall into cyclical thinking and to doom your future. To believe that you're star-crossed, and that the universe is against you. It'll be harder to wake up in the morning and to approach your daily tasks with eagerness.

But you must remember that this is temporary. Just as your happiness is transient, so, too, is your sorrow and heartache. You won't be down forever. Eventually, your heart will rebuild. It will patch all of its holes and its broken pieces together with renewed love and renewed hope. You will apply all of your lessons and color your vision with new perspectives and awareness.

Then, you will smile, as you realize that true wisdom cannot be attained and appreciated without the trials and the tribulations that form it. You need this pain. This suffering. It's your wake-up call that's going to remind you of what you deserve, and that will ensure that you do not settle in the future. It will also show you all of your breathtaking qualities. The very essences that illuminate the goodness in your soul and the resilience in your heart.

The tears will stop. The heartache will subside. The pain will leave. And in their wake, a newer, better you will be there. Smiling and appreciating everything that you've become.

It wasn't love that hurt you. It was your own expectations. Your own misapprehension and walls that pushed them away.

You build walls around your heart, and wonder why no one can enter. You scowl, and wonder why no one smiles back. You seal your lips, and wonder why no one opens up to you. Why you fail to explore the deepest depths of another's soul, where all the treasures reside and where you will find the real materials to build a meaningful, lasting connection.

You're afraid. You believe that love is the pain you were accustomed to. The hurtful words from your parents. The rejection from early school peers. The heartache from failed attempts. You live your life in a barricade, hoping that someone will finally give you a reason to leave. To embrace the world with open arms and a hopeful heart.

But it is your fears that are inhibiting you. Your old hurt that's permeating your mind. Love is not the cause of your sorrows. Nor is it the reason you're perpetually experiencing heartbreak and yearning for more. It is your tendency to avoid love. You overreact when someone wants to get too close, presuming the worst. Presuming that they are going to break into your heart, loot it for all its love and its joys, and abandon you in a prison of despair. You refuse to be transparent, fearing that your words will be used against you to exploit your weaknesses and to shame you for having needs. You stifle your voice, believing that your expressions will expel a lover, rather than actually grant them a chance to show up for you.

It is not love that's hurting you. It is you. It is your wounds resurfacing and deceiving you into believing that love is synonymous with pain, with heartbreak, and with devastation. It is you who is choosing to remain hidden, when so many are seeking your wondrous heart and your luminous soul.

You blame love, but in most cases, it is your self-fulling prophecies that are breaking your heart. Not love. Not them. Not anything else. Open yourself to new possibilities. Give people a chance to love, and to see you, in your entirety. You have so much beauty within. So much happiness to spread. But you're barricading yourself, shutting down, and not giving anyone the real you. That's why you often experience heartbreak, and why you attract the wrong people.

They lost, not you.

They lost someone who cared. Someone who offered every ounce of their heart and soul to make them smile. Who sacrificed hours of sleep to listen to their troubles, while offering comforting words and a solacing touch. Who took them into consideration, even when they could have taken advantage. Who compromised and advocated for their safety and security, even when they couldn't do it for themselves.

Someone who refused to give up on them. Who always saw their inner beauty, even when they were wallowing in their own rage. Even when they lost sight of themselves. Who took multiple opportunities to highlight their good qualities, and to show them how loved they were. Who provided a safe space where they could show their rawest, most vulnerable selves. Who showed them that love is not the pain and the hurt that they're used to, but a sanctuary that will honor their truest form.

They lost someone who loved them so purely, that they were willing to risk hurting their own precious, fragile heart. Who would have broken their backs carrying their burdens, if it meant granting them reprieve. Who pushed them to be better, irrespective of the obstacles present.

They lost. Not you. No, not with that loving heart of yours. Not with those kind eyes that see the greatness in others. With that resilient soul that refuses to quit, and that has the tenacity to love during the most trying times and the darkest days. Not with your pure character that holds firm to good values. That refuses to follow society's path of anger and hate. Not with your energy that invigorates every individual you encounter. They lost.

But you didn't. You're gaining an opportunity to take your heart, your inner light, and your vibrant soul to someone who will cherish it and recognize it for the divine blessing that it is. And that's why you can't surrender. That's why you can't give up.

It's time we dispel
our false notions. The
beliefs that our hurtful
environment instilled in
us. Because holding onto
them prevents us from
embracing the love, and
the lives, we deserve.

Many of us were lied to. Taught to believe that love would lead to heartache. That trusting others would lead to betrayal, pain, and humiliation. That opening up was dangerous and that showing people our vulnerabilities would grant them the chance to shame us and exploit our weaknesses. We were told to chase the "bigger" things. To pursue money, personal freedom, and a romantic partner that fits a certain mold. They must have a certain height, a certain body, and a certain ethnicity and faith for us to love them.

We're taught that if we defy the norms, we'll plummet. We'll incinerate our lives and the opportunities we're destined for. The blueprint has already been laid for us. The very path that led to prior failures, mediocrity, and destruction. But we're often too timid to venture toward anything new. To risk comfort for growth. Heartache for love. Failures for rewards.

And so we live believing in the worst. Thinking that people are unkind, cruel. That they're out to harm us and that we can never have true love and real meaning. That we must put up facades to gain acceptance. That we must follow the unfitting paths of those before us so that we can maintain comfort and stability. Leading the same lives and perpetuating generational trauma. A domino effect of causal heartbreaks and pain.

No more. It's time to be bold. To realize that we don't need to follow our family's or our environment's blueprints. We can pave our own paths. We can aspire for more. Because we deserve to experience the true fruits of love that only come when we're vulnerable. When we're ready to open our hearts to it, so that it may rush their insides with a cleansing light and a healing aura.

We can love someone who is different from us. Whose skin color and ethnicity differ. Who may hold some different beliefs. We can follow our hearts and acknowledge the truth that, although we cannot control who we fall for, we can choose to embrace a wholesome, inviting love. We can choose to see the goodness and appreciate how it blesses our lives.

Fear can't rule us. Because love is greater than it. Pain can't control us. Our desires far supersede it. We can receive what we're seeking. The right love is out there. Growth awaits us. And a life of improvement will, too. But we must first let go of everyone else's opinions so that we can honor our own.

It's hard to change. But you're going to get there. Little by little. Day by day. And in ways you've never imagined.

I often conflated difficulty with inability. I falsely believed that if I was struggling, then I wasn't meant to achieve my desired goal or change. I thought struggle was an indication that I was on the wrong path. An omen warning me that I needed to shift gears and head elsewhere. And any time a situation became too challenging, I'd despair and flee. I refused to stay, because I thought it was futile. I thought I'd end up wasting time and realize that I should have set my sights elsewhere. It was a vicious cycle of failed attempts, missed opportunities, and perpetual suffering,

Because no matter what path I undertook, I was still met with difficulty, struggle, and a nagging doubt that tried to cripple me. That's when my outlook changed. When I finally awoke from my slumber and discarded old associations.

Difficulty is not a sign that you're on the wrong path. Difficulty is an invitation for you to grow, to learn, and to change. It is never easy to embrace a new path. Your mind will swirl with uncertainty. Doubts will rise and tell you that you're incapable. That you're unfit for your intended outcomes, and that you're meant to fail and mourn your losses.

But it is your duty to overcome these challenges. To show up for yourself and to march through the doubts and the roughness, so that you can forge the new character, and the beautiful changes, you're seeking. Difficulties are obstacles designed to refine your character. To force you to examine yourself, and to improve the parts of you you've long neglected. So don't let them deter you. Don't let them decide your fate.

You can do what your mind says you cannot. You can grow even when old patterns continually resurface and try to affix you to a hurtful past and negative habits. You can rise even when you fall and feel hopeless. We are like diamonds; we need the pressure to form our shine and our greatness. Like seeds. We need the darkness of our difficulties and the waters of our efforts to finally sprout.

Difficulties were never designed to stop you, but to shape you into someone better. Someone who can step into the new role, the new power, and the new capabilities you've always been seeking. Keep going, and look forward to meeting the newest, best version of yourself. It's coming, and you'll be so thankful that you never quit. That you maintained your hope and fought to see better days.

A healthy relationship entails you being shown up for, irrespective of whatever you're going through. Because you shouldn't just be loved only when things are going right. You deserve to be loved through all of your challenges, your struggles, and your changes.

I thought love was performance-based. My relationships were stages where I had to put on the best acts. Where I thought that people required perpetual laughter, endless entertainment, and a facade of my infectious smiles and my energetic attitude. I couldn't fathom being loved while I struggled. While I flailed and could barely hang onto the edges of my sanity.

I based my present relationships off of my hurt past. Falsely thinking that if people saw the real me, in my purest state with my visible wounds and my insecurities, they'd use it all against me. That they'd mock me for having emotions and for being soft. Just as important people had during my youth and my more impressionable years.

My heart was clay: molded, carved, and indented by the painful words of those closest to me. I still see, and feel, the wounds. Wounds that glued my lips shut. Prevented me from giving life to my deepest thoughts and feelings. And I would fail to connect to others, because I was busy being who I thought I needed to be, and not who I actually was. I'd flash a smile when my soul was crying; I'd say I was fine when I really needed an ear to vent to and kind eyes to grant me hope; I'd prioritize others and their challenges when I was drowning and being buried beneath my own.

I thought relationships were dead ends. One-way streets where others were accommodated and bequeathed with my unrelenting efforts and my ascended energy. I didn't believe that I was worthy of being shown up for. I thought I was a burden. And I thought that if people saw the real me, it'd be exhausting and repulsive.

But the act was poisonous. The valleys of my heart needed the rain of authenticity. Yet I was feeding them with the toxins of falsity. And I couldn't go on any longer. I needed to be shown up for. So I finally allowed others in. Showed them my deepest wounds, my most embarrassing insecurities, and all of my shattered pieces. So that they could love me. So that I could be honored wholeheartedly.

And I hope this grants you the strength to do the same. A healthy relationship isn't a space for you to give, without ever receiving. For you to suffocate beneath the weight of others' expectations. For you to drown while you keep others afloat. A healthy relationship is a spacious home possessing enough room for your challenges, your difficulties, your fears, and your doubts. It possesses the room for you to lay your barest aspects, and to receive the exact same love, commitment, and devotion you give out.

If you're struggling to be real, something is off. Either you're with the wrong person or you're too fearful to unveil your truest self. Make the change, and start living authentically. Start presenting others with the opportunity to love you, so that you may heal, thrive, and gain a loving, meaningful relationship. The kind that you saw in movies, but were taught to disbelieve in, so you never aspired for it.

They may love you. But
if they can't choose you,
you must walk away.
You are way too valuable
to linger and to wait.
And you deserve to be
chosen unconditionally.

Oftentimes, you don't feel worthy because you're wait-ing for another to choose you. And when you wait for another to choose you, you're essentially telling your mind, your heart, and your soul that they require external validation. That they are inadequate, and will remain so, until another's love and selection colors them with more worth and more vibrance.

And the longer you do this, the more worthless you'll feel. The bigger your void will grow. And the more you'll end up chasing people, and relationships, that were never meant to be caught, because they do not align with your deeper purpose, and the love that you deserve. And you'll eventually see that you can never fill your soul with other people's love and acceptance. You can only do it with your own.

And that begins when you stop chasing. When you refuse to settle for those who won't show up for you. Who won't gift you with the same love, admiration, and kindness you gift them with. When you will no longer occupy spaces that demand you to be someone you're not, that demand you to stifle your emotionality; to bite your tongue and say only what you believe they want to hear; to hide your thoughts and your needs and shrink yourself, so that you may conveniently fit into their expectations.

You deserve to be chosen unconditionally. And that means unconditionally choosing yourself, and setting an example, by speaking your mind, no longer settling, and honoring your needs—even when that entails letting go of others and breaking your own heart. Choosing yourself is where your healing starts, and where you will gain opportunities to have the right love.

You're not a failure just because something didn't work out. You're beautifully brave and beautifully bold for giving your all, even though you know you could get hurt. That's why you're worthy, and why you should never give up.

Y ou're not a failure just because they left. Just because your heart is broken. Because you loved so openly, purely, and honestly, yet were still met with another's inability to choose you.

You're not a failure because you chose the wrong one. Because you invested so heavily into someone, even when warnings appeared. Even when you knew better.

You're not a failure just because they ended up with someone else. Because they cannot see your worth and match all that you give. Because they couldn't connect themselves to your smile, your ways of love, and your finer qualities.

You're not a failure just because you've tried building love with others, and it has collapsed. Because you're "different," and you struggle to jive with society's masses.

You're not a failure. You're human. You're normal. You're a traveler experiencing a wide array of differing sceneries, peoples, and experiences. And this is the path you must embark on to learn, to grow, and to determine who you truly are, and who you would like to become.

And it's beautiful that you have the courage to undertake such a journey. That you refuse to cower to your fears, and that you rise above your pain with the hope that your life can change, and that you will eventually find what you're seeking and become who you desire. You trudge forward, even through your doubts, your heartache, and your despair.

You're learning. And learning involves mistakes. But mistakes do not diminish your worth. They add to your wisdom, and to your ability to improve. Give yourself less hate, and more love. Less criticism, and more positive acknowledgment. You try, even when it'd be easier to quit. Even when you feel you can't progress. You see the goodness, and you believe in the infinite possibilities for something better. That is half the battle—and you make it look easy. Your perspective is key.

Where you see darkness and failure, there is so much light and encouragement. You could easily become bitter and allow your heart to harden. Yet you choose to remain committed to love, to growth, and to genuine connection. That's why you're an inspiration, and why you shouldn't ever quit.

Your love is your strength. Not your weakness. And though your journey can be trying and excruciating, you are making your way toward the changes and the life you want. These moments are your guidance, leading you forward, even when it doesn't seem that way.

They left you, because
it's easier for them to
be with someone who
doesn't make them face
their emotions. Someone
who doesn't challenge
them to grow. Your
love is powerful, and
only the right ones will
be able to handle it.

Your love is a shovel. Excavating deeply into the most tender, intricate parts of another's soul. It finds the gems they've long suppressed—holds them tightly, kindly, and lovingly. Shows them that they have nothing to fear. But some are unprepared to show their truest selves, because they think the worst of others.

Your love is a high-tech scanning system, detecting the best in others. Valuing them for qualities, tendencies, and traits that they've always wanted to be seen for. Detecting their most intimate difficulties so that you may aid them and offer rest during their tiresome travels. But some do not believe that there is any good for you to detect and enjoy.

It is a mighty ship that can handle the roughest seas and their tumultuous storms and currents. Able to carry them from the shores of heartache to the land of love. Where they will heal, expand, and bloom into the freshest rose awaiting the right hands to hold them as their renewed fragrance permeates the land. But some do not think they're worthy of such scenery, so they fight to stay where they feel comfortable.

It is a gentle hand, carrying them through the most intimidating terrains. A hand that doesn't tremble when the load is heavy. That doesn't collapse when darkness approaches. It holds them and pushes them forward, even when they're terrified and doubtful. But some disbelieve that your kindness will persist, thinking that it is a mere act bound to cease eventually.

Your love is a gift. But your love is like a tree. It will never grow properly without the right soil and the right land. You cannot plant your love in a barren, unprepared heart. In a heart that is blinded by fears and a stubborn unwillingness to change. Your love needs the right hands to hold it. The right eyes to recognize it. The right soul to house it and to water it with reciprocity. That is when you will finally realize that most of the time, it wasn't about you. It was about who you were choosing.

Love can be hard to accept. Especially when another doesn't believe that they are worthy of it, or that they deserve a healthy connection. Especially when your love defies the hurt, the mistreatment, and the conditional circumstances another has been used to. People will struggle to appreciate a love that opposes what they've known their whole lives. They will also struggle to accept it when all they've been used to is hurt and disappointment. That is their work. Not you. You were doing it right all along. But you were devoting yourself to others who weren't ready. That never invalidates your love, but merely shows that you should reassess who you're giving it to.

Someday, you will see that you aren't the problem. Your love is beautiful, and your intentions are pure. But you're giving your all to the wrong people, and that's why it's breaking you.

There are other truths that your pain is concealing and causing you to misinterpret. You think that your love is insufficient—that no matter what you do, you'll never be good enough. But there are so many reasons that someone cannot accept your love and build a meaningful relationship with you.

Sometimes, it's because they are too wounded. Their pain fogs their vision, and they cannot recognize a healthy love with a heartfelt connection. They then choose others who fit their comfort of familiar pains and trauma bonds, who keep them feeling secure because change and growth are far too daunting.

Sometimes, they're unprepared to step into the space of inner evolution that your love is demanding for a long-lasting relationship. It is easier to flee and to make excuses than it is to work on themselves and to acknowledge their hurt.

Many people do not trust love. They exist in paradigms of hurt and betrayal. So they project their insecurities onto you. That is not your fault. Nor can you force them to change. You're naturally worthy, and you deserve to be easily recognized and shown up for.

And it's time that you start giving your all to the ones who reciprocate. The ones who are willing to match your efforts, even as doubts, fears, and challenges arise. Even as the urges to flee are strong. You overcome your challenges to give great love. It's time you encourage others to do the same.

Uncertainty is a blessing.
It can lead to new paths
and new opportunities.
But most of the time,
we're too afraid to trust
and to open ourselves
to newness. That's why
we're stuck fighting the
same patterns and dealing
with the same things.

New opportunities are terrifying. Your mind concocts images of everything that could go wrong. You imagine scowling faces, scathing insults, and embarrassing failures that are going to shatter your confidence and send you packing back to your familiar, stagnant comfort zone.

You also paint the present with your past hurt. Believing that the outcomes will be the same, and that trying is pointless. You're tempted to stay where your fears say that you belong. In the expectations of others. In the spaces that they've relegated you to. In the areas they've carved out, so that you're not controversial and you're appeasing their comfort.

It is not the world that is scary. It is your perception of it. New opportunities are terrifying, yes. But they're also blessings. Uncertainty holds the chances for you to gain so much. For you to finally do something different and to grow in unprecedented ways.

Do not only see the risk. Start to look at the rewards. At the treasure chests housing new growth, new love, and new moments for you to prosper and rise. Just as easily as you could fail and be hurt, you could succeed and be grateful that you were bold enough to try.

Perhaps these new chances are everything you've been waiting for. Perhaps they'll allow you to meet a new lover.

One who protects your soul, cultivates it with kindness, and bestows an all-encompassing warmth upon you.

Perhaps this new job will be everything you're seeking. One that maximizes your skillset and enables you to achieve your financial goals. That grants you a kind, comfortable work environment where you can feel more appreciated and be better compensated for your work.

Perhaps this new path, along with these new decisions, will form you into the person you've always wanted to be. One who's mentally stronger and stands firm for what you want, even though others may disagree. Who's more open and has healthier expectations and self-love, so that you're not chasing the wrong people and the wrong things. Who's more vocal, so that you can express your needs and determine who's capable of fulfilling them.

New opportunities aren't the destruction your mind is depicting. They are often the chances you've been needing. The roads that lead to somewhere new. Somewhere that holds the light, the love, and the transformations you're worthy of. Take the chances and believe in opportunism. Goodness awaits. Blessings are there. Change is calling to you. But they need your bravery before they'll reveal themselves.

Heartbreak is exactly what you need. Because it's the only catalyst powerful enough to spark your desire to change, and to initiate something new.

You often curse heartbreak. Declaring it your end. Your unbecoming and your inner destruction. And to a certain degree, you're correct. It is your ending, your unbecoming, and your inner destruction.

But it is also your new beginning, your becoming, and your rebirth. You needed this heartbreak. You needed something so powerful, so mighty, to wake you up and galvanize you into action. Because you wouldn't be motivated with it.

You'd be confined to mediocrity. To a lover who wasn't going to show up for you, prioritize your needs, and love you in the ways that you love them. You'd stick around, continuing to give pieces of yourself until there was nothing left. Until you were broken and left to believe that this is all you're meant for.

Yet now you have the fuel. You're tired of feeling hurt and of dealing with the same relational ineptitude. You're tired of not satisfying your soul's inner cries for more. You know that you deserve better. And now that this relationship has died, you can regain your sense of self and connect to the inner you. To the deep love you harbor and the wide expanse your soul possesses.

This heartbreak is one end. But it is not the end. Not your complete end. It is your beginning. Your golden opportunity to reframe how you see yourself. To give your heart, your soul, and your energy the precious attention, warmth, and kindness that they deserve. For you to start a new relationship, down the road, that is healthy and beautiful.

This heartbreak is your becoming. This is when you will dive deeply into your own soul and realize the gems you've long possessed. The relics of wisdom, the portraits of beauty, and the diamonds of kindness that shine and captivate those who recognize what they truly are. This is when you will kindly tuck your painful past away and embrace something new. Something that repairs your self-worth and your confidence. This is when you will empower yourself to live authentically, and to share who you truly are with pride.

This is your rebirth. You will take the debris from your broken heart and build a firmer character. One that honors your deepest principles, and which refuses to be molded by fear, heartache, and self-sacrifice. That will speak up for your needs, stand up to others when they mistreat you, and that will demand better. No longer will you be a statue, mute and unmoving. They will never find you where they left you. You will take your ashes, plant them into the ground, and watch a new version of yourself emerge. You will build the new with all of the old.

Then, you will be thankful for this heartache. Because without it, you wouldn't be who you are today. You wouldn't have been pushed to change. You would have kept settling. But now, you'll be different. And you'll finally smile and have what you've always deserved.

Sometimes, you're the one who bids farewell. The one who breaks another's heart. Don't be so hard on yourself. Be proud that you're strong enough, and selfless enough, to do what's right, even if it entails breaking your own heart.

Sometimes, you're the villain in another's story. The one who broke their heart, who ran away, and who couldn't give them what they wanted and deserved. And it'll be hard to stomach this. Hard to imagine that when they reflect upon pain and heartache, you will come to mind. You will be the cause. The force that disrupted them and left them in shambles.

But still, it is ok. You're human, and you will make mistakes. Sometimes, you'll leave when it's too soon. When you're on the cusp of building something great. Sometimes, you'll hurt others. You'll let your anger consume you and you'll leave cracks and bruises. Sometimes, you'll fail to be there for others, as you're busy trying to save yourself. Trying to salvage the little bits of you that are left.

Yet these moments are just as needed as all of the others. They teach you compassion. Grant you the ability to be softer, kinder, so that you may empathize with others during their trying times and encourage them to be better.

You are not a perfectly designed character in a heroic novel. You're human. You're real. Authentic. Carrying imperfections, flaws, and mistakes that make you wonderful in ways you may struggle to see. Yes, you are flawed and imperfect.

But at least you're not selfish and uncaring. Cruel and callous. You are open, loving, and strong. You value others, the way they may not value you. You prioritize the preservation of their hearts and the upkeep of their emotions. Your kindness is the reason that this world maintains its goodness and its peace. Your ways prevent the flames of hatred and hurt from engulfing anyone.

Maybe you're a villain to the ones you've hurt. To the people who do not understand your emotional depth. A depth that will overtake oceans and fill galaxies. But you're a hero to yourself and to the rest of the world, for honoring what others deserve, and for lovingly pursuing what fits your love, your heart, and your passions.

You deserve to appreciate yourself for not only removing yourself once you've realized that you're unfit for another, but for also valuing your wants and your needs. Many people exclude their wants and their desires. Yet you don't. You know that you matter, too. And you won't settle until both you, and another, receive what you both deserve.

Forgive yourself for the
times you went forward
when you shouldn't have.
The times you stayed,
when you should have
left. And all the times
you settled for less than
you deserved, and for
hurting others. You're
human, and these mistakes
will make you better.

Forgive yourself for the times you stayed, even when you shouldn't have. When your heart begged you to leave, as your conscience continued telling you, and showing you, why you were going to be hurt. You wanted to believe in the good of others, and it cost you your peace and your sanity. And that's ok.

Forgive yourself for the times you ran away from love. You were too hurt to believe that it could offer any good and that it could gently fit into your life. You ran to save yourself, only to end up in more pain and more misery. And that's ok.

Forgive yourself for hurting others. For saying and doing the wrong things. Insulting them. Yelling at them. And disgracing them whenever they upset you. You wanted to send a message and appease your ego. And that's ok.

Forgive yourself for not taking a stand to defend yourself and your needs. It was easier to stay quiet than it was to confront your fears and to potentially get shut down. You were hanging on by threads; another hurtful word could have broken you then. You didn't want to subject yourself to more heartache. And that's ok.

Forgive yourself for going with the crowd. Getting submerged in societal expectations as your inner voice faded into the background. You wanted acceptance, and that's how you thought you'd get it. You were tired of not fitting in. Even a moment of inclusion felt better than your inner turmoil. And that's ok.

Forgive yourself for sacrificing your needs, and being someone you weren't, to receive love. Love is the sun we all wish to bask in. You wanted a dose of it, to finally feel the goodness you felt you've been deprived of. And that's ok.

Forgive yourself for everything. You're human. That critical voice in your head isn't yours. You're worth more than your failures, your heartbreaks, and your struggles. You're a beautiful compilation of attained wisdom merged with human softness and a gentle kindness. These experiences taught you and added to your greatness. You don't need to indict yourself and condemn yourself to a lifetime of regret.

You deserve to let go. To be free. To soar the skies of new opportunities, and to love the person who has endured insufferable grief and unspeakable traumas. To credit yourself for continuing. You are not who you were then. There's no need to relive those times. To wallow in sorrows and to shame yourself. You've changed and you've grown. And you owe it to everything that broke you in the past.

Thank you for loving me, through all of my struggles and my challenges. For standing beside me, and lifting me, when I felt I couldn't go on.

Thank you for loving me. For seeing my goodness, and my sincerity, lying beneath my fears and my insecurities. For understanding that all of the times I was hurt and I lashed out, it wasn't about you. It was about my wounds. I'm accustomed to feeling forgotten and left out. So I often expect the worst in others. Believing that abandonment is inevitable. That heartbreak is an insidious predator lurking and waiting to catch me spontaneously. Yet you do not wield this against me. Whereas others may chain another in their faults and their flaws, you set me free. Using the keys of your kindness to liberate me, so that I may progress.

Whenever I am distant and detached, you meet me with love. With closeness. With a hand that invites me forward. An embrace that sweeps my sorrows, my anxieties, and my disquiet away. Your smile is one thousand stars compiled into one massive, effervescent guiding light. A light I rely on, and would certainly stray without.

Whenever I falter, or struggle to be positive as I'm toiling for more, you encourage me. Planting love deep into my core. Watering my ears with support and warming words. Telling me and showing me that you love me, so that I do not feel alone and neglected on this cold, difficult path. I'm used to being judged for my struggles and my challenges. I assume that people in my present will assume the worst like many did in my past.

But not you. You always see the best in me. Where I feel like a failure for not doing more, you see a man who cares and who prioritizes striving for excellence. Where I believe I am not enough, you admire my ambition and remind me that my mere pursuit of greatness and improvement suffices. You refuse to let me degrade myself.

And that is why I am eternally grateful for you. Why, whenever I bow my head in submission to God, I am certain to mention your name and to praise Him for you: His ultimate blessing; His mercy manifested; and His kindness reflected in soft eyes, a tender smile, and a warm frame. A woman who exemplifies compassion and strength in laudable ways.

Life will look different
when you finally get
to where you want
to be. It'll be hard to
accept. Don't allow
your thoughts and your
unrealistic expectations
to ruin your present joy.

I have the hardest time enjoying the present. I'm either too busy reminiscing about the past or worrying about the future. I'm constantly trying to mold the present to fit into my mind's inflated, exaggerated ideas of happiness, elation, and success. I need that high. That surge of energy that overtakes my veins and puts me on top of the world.

Yet I forget that my lofty expectations are often underpinned by my childhood traumas and my fears of being hurt. That high that I'm seeking is a version of past dysfunction where I never had a safe middle ground. Where it was either chaos or turmoil. Those unrealistic expectations are faulty foundations I'm walking on because I am trying so hard to avoid the pain that was etched into me early on. The very pain that makes me doubt happiness's existence, and if I'll ever become who I want to be.

We all do this, don't we? Entertain the unrealistic because we're terrified of becoming what we escaped. Chase the highs and the extremes because we still haven't realized that that's what we've been accustomed to during our old traumas and woundings. And then we end up hurt and dissatisfied, because we miss out on enjoying and cultivating the special moments we're being blessed with. That's what I do.

I miss out on the moments where kind eyes are burrowing into mine, finally seeing me for all that I am. On the soft lips that implant love into my deepest parts, inviting me to let go of my pain. To finally accept what I've long yearned for, but struggled to believe I deserved. The warm embraces that shelter me and allow me to feel human, and not like I'm an emotionless, sex-craved maniac that society often depicts us men as. The warm words that soothe my broken parts and gently aid me in putting them back together.

I've finally realized that happiness isn't the exaggerations my mind concocts—most of which are built on fears, other people's expectations, and on trauma. Nor is it what other people define for me. Happiness is truly enjoying the present and accepting that it can be different from what

I've expected—perhaps even better, if I open myself and my heart, and I allow it to be. That it can divert from the course that my elders taught me. It can be what I want it to be, provided I am being a good man, leading a truthful, God-conscious life, and enjoying the simple blessings.

Like her. With her elegance, her radiance, and her loving hugs that rationalize every ounce of hurt I've endured. Like my prayer rug that enables me to come broken, imperfect, and hurt, yet I still can seek God's light and His mercy. Like the sunlight that dances upon my skin and reminds me that, although I am struggling and hurting, and although the future scares me, I am alive. I am not six feet beneath the ground. I have faculties that allow me to enjoy this divine gift of creation.

Yes, your happiness will look different. You will end up with a different lover. A different mindset. A different path that you never could have imagined. But it can still be everything you need, you want, and you deserve. Give it a chance. Step out of your mind, and step into your life. You deserve this. I deserve this. And we can enjoy it and take it as it comes.

Be thankful for the good
that you have. It could
always be worse. And
someday, you will regret
having not appreciated
all the beauty and the joy
around you, as you were
too busy focusing on your
worries and your concerns.

We miss out on current joy and happiness because we're fixated on our fears and our worries. We spend so much time being troubled over scenarios that have not happened and may not even happen. We conjure these fictional tales and get so invested in them that we sully our happiness.

We calculate how we'll handle a situation if it potentially goes downward. How we'll respond if a certain individual sees us at a family, or work, function, and intends on insulting us. We ruminate over our unborn children and worry about who they'll end up marrying, how they'll believe or disbelieve in God, and what the world will be like then. We fear that our spouse's love may disappear within a few years, and then we're busy envisioning ourselves heartbroken, abandoned, lost, and determining how we'll split the assets.

We fear that our new job will be overwhelming. That we'll never be able to grasp the new systems, or fit in with our new coworkers. We're busy envisaging them being unkind to us, thus making us feel detached and lonesome. We then contemplate if we're actually making the right decision, and if we might end up missing our previous job and wanting to go back.

Everything seems so dire in our minds. We then become riddled with anxiety. Lost in layers of thoughts projecting catastrophic endings, irremediable heartbreaks, and endless sadness. And then, we base our realities on these fantasies.

We lash out at our significant other, fearing that their fatigue-based silence is an early, subtle manifestation of their impending disinterest and their eventual termination of love. We go into that new job with coldness and aloofness because we're already certain that others are going to dislike us and be rude. We refuse to take chances because we've already convinced ourselves that the worst is the reality, and that it's better to stay within our comfort zones.

Then, our cold, erratic behavior pushes our significant other away. Our overreactions leave no room for their explanations, nor for genuine, warm bonding. We deepen the distance—even though we know we're contributing to it. We then tell ourselves that if they really cared, they'd close the gap—when they've tried to countless times. But our reluctance repelled them. Eventually, they do conclude that ties must be severed. And our worst fears have materialized.

We go into that new job thinking we're inadequate, and that others have already decided to dislike us. We then struggle to grow in the new role because we're busy believing we're inept. We also struggle to form ties with the new colleagues, because they're keeping their distance, misinterpreting our fears and insecurities as arrogance and disinterest. We then continue feeling isolated. Eventually, we start missing our old jobs and we quit before we could have grown and done something professionally remarkable.

We end up feeling depressed and purposeless, because we never took chances to explore new territories and new opportunities that could have softened our hearts with kind smiles, loving souls, and lifelong inner growth. We let our fears win, watching them wave their flags within the bases of our hearts. The bases we've always wanted to claim, so that we could wave our own flags displaying colors of our resilience, our determination, and our relentless strength.

And this shows that sometimes, it isn't others. It isn't our exes, our bad bosses, or our upbringings. It is what we feed ourselves, and how we react, that determines our outcomes. We can have our fears—but we don't need to respond to them. Nor must we live in our minds. Every fear is a possibility, but still could be very improbable.

Maybe your significant other will stop wanting to be with you. Or maybe they won't. Maybe they'll never tire of exploring your wondrous depths, and basking in your marvelous inner light. Of voyaging through the seas of your compassion and the waves of your knowledge. Maybe they'll love you even more by then, because you'll both have grown through your challenges, your tribulations, and all of the good times. Maybe you'll both be examples of what a healthy, happy marriage is. Maybe others will look upon you and glean hope for their own situations.

Maybe your new job will be lackluster and your new co-workers will dislike you. Or maybe it'll end up being the perfect vessel for your professional ascension. Maybe your coworkers will be the kindest, softest individuals you've met, who will end up adding more joy and humor to your day.

Maybe those new opportunities will fail and shake your confidence. Or maybe they'll be everything you're looking for. Maybe they won't be what you want, but what you need. Bringing you to new experiences, new individuals, and new moments that demolish your soul's old walls of pain, so that you may welcome love, light, and happiness again. Maybe they will show you the hidden beauties within yourself, and introduce you to moments that'll make you feel alive and transform you wonderfully.

Life is always risky. But that doesn't erase its beauty or its goodness. It's time that we not only remember this, but that we enact our purpose and we embrace the world with all of our love, our goodness, and our light. Because that's where we'll yield change, and how we'll finally attain what we deserve.

It's time we love people for who they are, and not for what they own or possess; for the ways in which they treat us and support us, and not for the titles they hold. True love is unconditional, and when we open ourselves up to it, we realize that it transcends what we were taught.

Many are looking for love in the wrong places. Seeking it in another's wallet. In their job position. In the backseat of their car or within one of the rooms in their mansions. In a perfect smile or a perfect body that stimulates their hormones. In the same ethnicity, religion, or belief system. In their societal titles and the supposed prestige they flash.

But love is too precious to be mediocre. To be confined to the whimsical, trivial fancies of materialism and the unrealistic expectations many have been inundated with. Love is not material. It will never be found in another's wealth or their possessions. Love is infinite. It cannot be chained to skin colors, ethnicities, and religion. Love is accepting. It sees someone for who they truly are, and not who society is telling them that they must be. Love is an extension of God. Undying. Merciful. Endless. And all-encompassing. It does not run disintegrate as another's wealth and looks do.

We're searching for it incorrectly. Assuming that it must be what everyone tells us, or that there's a certain checklist we need, where an individual must be everything we want. Love is too real to be a fairytale that trivializes it and diminishes it.

And it's time that we love people as they are. For their qualities and their traits. Not their acquisitions and their statuses.

For the kind hearts that reside within them, and not the bra sizes and the defined chest muscles hiding them.

For the sweet, encouraging words they nourish us with, and not the plump, desirous lips they come out of, which our lusts impel us toward.

For the hands that lift us up when we're down and struggling, and not the watches, rings, or bracelets adorning them.

For the nurturing soft eyes that see the best in us during our darkest days, and not their specific color we're infatuated with.

For the faces that softly press themselves against us to express love, tenderness, and affection, and not their geometric structures we believe are needed and perfect.

For the money that is spent to heal us, grant us stability, and to show their commitment to building a meaningful, safe future, and not the overall amount in their bank accounts.

For the legs that walk toward us openly and supportively, and that will walk through fire to see us smile and succeed, and not their shapes that have a certain appeal.

Love, and be loved, for the right reasons, and you will have a fruitful, lasting relationship. One that holds a space for your authenticity and your growth. That acknowledges your greatness and doesn't require you to be someone, or something you're not. One that believes in you, and wants what's genuinely best. That is true love. And it exceeds the societal impositions we've been subjected to.

I may struggle to show my
love, but I promise you,
it's there. It's like gravity:
you may not see it, but its
force is responsible for all
of this stability and order.
You will not always feel
it, but my heart burns
and gallops because of it.
I love you, and you will
fully accept it eventually.

Sometimes, I may seem distant and detached. As if I am lost and unhappy. But that is not the full story. I experience chapters, my love. Chapters involving sadness, fears, and sorrows—which have nothing to do with you or anyone else. I have the bad tendency to create problems and to fixate on them because I'm terrified of being hurt. Of being trapped and feeling inadequate—things I often felt in my childhood.

Yet these struggles are a blessing. They've allowed me to see, and experience, our love for one another. A love that draws tears from my eyes. That opens the gates of my heart and flushes every ounce of its pain and its worries. That highlights qualities I never knew I possessed. It has shown me your undying commitment and devotion. Your indomitable strength that stands beside me, no matter how much I struggle and falter. Your eyes that see the best in me as I work to become even better. Your soft tone that's a compass directing me toward safety and peace, when I am lost and uncertain. Your heart that beats with goodness and tenderness, and that always offers me stability when I'm distressed and endangered.

These struggles have shown me our devotion to one another, and to this beautiful, loving relationship. I am blessed to have this, and I hope you know that I sing your praises constantly. I love you. There is no one else I'd rather be with. I cannot imagine my life without you and the infinite blessings that have come. My grandmother once told me that women are either good luck or bad luck. I laughed when she said that. But I do see what she meant. Because you have brought so much good luck into my life. So many opportunities and blessings that I am grateful for.

But none of them are greater than your mere presence, and the ability to love you, enjoy you, and grow in this union. My love is so great for you that I often fixate on the potential of pain. And that is where I must do my work. Because there is always a risk. A situation can either succeed or fail. I want to learn to see the potential reward and the bright side, rather than the potential failure and the fears.

And that is why I will always go forward. Against my fears, my doubts, my worries. Against my anxieties and the years of trauma telling me to avoid love. Because you're worth it. And a life with you, your smile, and your warmth is far greater than a life without it. I would rather burn and crash with you by my side, than to live a life of comfort and ease without you. I will conquer my challenges and my fears, so that I can love you better, and show that I appreciate you endlessly. You are the love of my life and you are everything I could have ever hoped to have and more. I love you, baby. Thank you for everything.

I'm not used to being loved right. I fear abandonment. And that's why I unintentionally push people away. But I'm healing. And I promise: someday, I'm going to give you a love that'll be better than anything before it.

I tend to assume the worst in others. Thinking that any-thing I say will be used against me. Where people aren't simply friends, or a lover isn't simply a lover, but where everyone is a judge, waiting to wield my words against me and to exploit my weaknesses, so that they may condemn me to a life of agony. One where I am forced to suffer for every wrong statement and misdeed.

That's why I'm quick to overreact. Why my mouth is a raised drawbridge and my heart is a fortress guarded by painful memories and secrecy. I often felt that I couldn't be myself, and that the sides that I did show had to be reminiscent of what others wanted.

Yet all I craved was love. I wanted to feel like I belonged. Like I mattered and could be held safely, lovingly, and tenderly, as I walked another through my heartache and my wounds. I never wanted to withhold my most intimate parts. The very essences that show my masculine softness and my vulnerabilities.

But it can be hard for me to trust. And that is why I pre-sume the worst. Why I overreact and prematurely end things. I have unintentionally broken my heart so many times, because I assumed another would do it. I assumed that the very moment I shared a secret, or showed a gentle side, that I'd be judged, unloved, and abandoned.

I still subconsciously believe that love is conditional. Which is why I condition my efforts, my vulnerabilities, and my openness. I know that I can be closed off. That I can withhold the very oxygen of transparency that every relationship needs to survive.

And for that, I am sorry. It's not you. It's me and my fears. My assumptions that every storm will wash you away and eject you toward something better. That every mistake will cost me your love. Every wrong word or misused opportunity will shatter your hope in me and lower my status in your precious, loving eyes.

But I'm learning. Silence and inaction are not the answers. They merely fulfill my outmoded expectations and rob me of the opportunity to improve and create a meaningful union with you. So I express myself, I love hard, and I open up in the most vulnerable ways. That's what you deserve, and this is what we need, so that we may strengthen our blessed connection.

And the more I heal, the more I will love you. The harder I will protect you. The deeper I will go for you, for us, and for our future family, God willing. I will grant you a love better than anything you've ever experienced. A love so pure and wholesome, that it will rewrite your wrongs, raise your soul, and show you that fairytales aren't fairytales after all, but a reality that you've always deserved.

She's there, waiting for you to build a meaningful, loving relationship, where the two of you can open your hearts, come together, and spend a lifetime in love. But she can't do it on her own. You must be willing to give, so the two of you can become a unit.

Give her your love, and she will give you her compassion. Her listening ears, her soft words, and her tender heart that will remedy your troubles and mirror your strength back to you, so that you may continue. She won't let you fall or fail. She'll push you forward, even when you're afraid and uncertain.

Give her your heart, and she will give you freedom. The full reign to be your truest, most vulnerable self, where you will receive the love, the acceptance, and the support you've always desired. She will take all of its fragments and make new spaces of beauty and inclusion. She will plant love in each of its corridors. She will ensure that it feels like the finest relic, encased in a safe room where its splendor can remain intact and captivate onlookers.

Give her your openness, and she will give you acceptance. She will make fairytales out of your nightmares. She will remind you of your worth, as you struggle to pull yourself up. She will show you that you have nothing to be ashamed of. That you're bold and strong for continuing, while many others would have quit.

Give her your honesty, and she will give you her wisdom. Words that will show you that you aren't your past hurt, nor are you worthless for having struggles and falling short. She will show you that the very aspects you dislike about yourself, are the same aspects that make you who you are, and that show your kindness, your care, and your genuineness. She will always see the best in you.

Give her your soul, and she will give you a home inside yourself. She will paint its rooms with colors of love, adoration, and warmth. She will rebuild your inner brokenness and revive your belief in your purpose. She will take your weaknesses and love them as if they are your greatest strengths.

Give her your fears, the horror stories your mind plays, and the shaking you feel when you want to go after your dreams, and she will give you her strength. She will allow you to stand on her uplifting insights and her undying belief in you. You will be renewed again.

Give her your deepest hopes, and she will give you a future. She will take your strengths, your purpose, and your ambition, and build a vibrant, passionate life with you. She will set you upon the best paths, where the light brushes your skin, the wind guides you toward your greatest abilities, and the world smiles upon you, as it lauds your capabilities. She will rewrite your past. You will feel grateful for enduring every morsel of pain and struggle. For they will have led you toward her and her life-changing love.

Give her everything you possess. There is no other way to love her, and no other way to tap into her gifts. She's everything you want, you need, and you could be blessed with. But you must open yourself to the possibility of being loved right. Otherwise, you'll miss out.

Tell them you love them. Express yourself. Life is too short for you to wait around, to entertain the what-ifs, and to miss out on what you deserve. Start showing the real you, so that you can embrace your greater purpose and experience a better love.

You're scared to open your heart and to show them how deeply, and how passionately, you love them. You recount the times you've been hurt and were left yearning for so much more. You're worried that they don't share the same feelings, and that they will run at the first sight of your impassioned, unbridled love and care. You wait for them to be the first one.

But you've done this before, haven't you? Invalidated yourself by refusing to breathe life into your words. Allowed heartfelt expressions to wither away in the back of your throat, while they eagerly awaited the chance to leap from your lips and to show another how cherished and how valued they are. Fed your sense of worthlessness by saying that your feelings are inconsequential—although you'd suddenly recognize their purpose the moment another expressed themselves.

You've watched, waited, and suppressed your feelings countless times. You've deprived yourself of genuine, meaningful connections, because you feel that fear is more powerful than love. But it won't always be that way. The past cannot define your future, if you choose to be different. Your pain is not who you are. You're worth more than that.

And it's time that you express yourself. That you stop waiting, and you start living. Be the one who goes first. Your emotions deserve to be expressed. To be heard, witnessed, and felt in ways that change others' lives, as you see that you always deserved to share them. Society can be too cold and too closed. Be the difference.

You can finally gain what you're seeking by courageously going forward. Breaking down your own inner walls, and allowing your love to flood the desolate plains of hearts everywhere. Allowing your warmth to permeate cold souls and to grant life in their darkest, most remote depths. Your initiation could be the very catalyst that will inspire another to share their feelings about you. And even if they aren't mutual, you'd still have validated your emotions and set yourself free from someone who can't honor what you need and you deserve.

You're too precious to wait around. You can go first. You can be bold enough to disclose your warmest thoughts and your most passionate expressions. They'll always guide you toward what you're worthy of. And they'll finally show you that your feelings, your needs, and your emotional depths matter, and that your boldness will inspire others to change, too.

We believe that settling
with one person will rob
us of many experiences.
We're too busy listening
to the masses and
believing that marriage
is a prison sentence, and
not an opportunity to
experience unprecedented
love, beautiful growth,
and a lifetime of bliss.

The idea of commitment once terrified me. I felt like I'd be trapped. Forced to deal with the monotony of marriage, the mundane routine that'd make me crave my old life of youthful exuberance and the freedom to only worry about myself.

But deep within me, I craved long-term affection, devotion, love, and connection. We all do. Yet we allow our painful pasts and our upbringings to deter us. We color our perception with other people's opinions and ideals. That was my mistake.

I based marriage off of what I had seen in my younger years. The arguing. The yelling. The uncompromising personalities who refused to work through issues and grow. I felt lonely, trapped, and fearful. I conflated marriage with the chaos and the dissatisfaction I witnessed. I didn't understand that there were other ways. That I could be different—a word that often unsettled many around me and had multiple negative associations affixed to it.

I'd run from love and allow these negative associations to reel me away. But I'm now learning that marriage, and commitment, can be beautiful enterprises offering hope, growth, joy, and divine love. A relationship doesn't need to be the fighting and the conflict I'm exposed to. Nor must commitment entail misery, mundaneness, and monotony.

People change and they grow. They will not be the same today as they were yesterday. Nor the same a year from now. And loving you has shown me that. I have seen you in a multitude of ways. When you're happy. You're sad. You're hopeful and cheerful. When you're down, irritated, and annoyed. When you're determined, eager, and set. You are never the same. You're constantly growing, changing, and evolving. It's breathtaking to witness, and it affords me the chance to love you differently, in new, exhilarating ways.

I have watched you become a marvelous professional. One who commands respect, who has a firm grasp on knowledge, and who teaches me things about the business world I never would have contemplated. It is enchanting to learn from you and to see your progress.

I have watched you become more expressive. Before, you wouldn't open up much. You would bottle your emotions and carry on, even though I knew you'd be boiling inside. Now, you confidently, boldly, and smoothly express yourself. You show me the gentlest sides of your heart and the enchanting wonders of your soul. You gift me with your wisdom, and it leaves lasting impressions.

I have watched you become a sweeter lover. You were always kind and compassionate. But now, you're more open to commitment, to marriage, and to how enjoyable life can be when we're together. Your warmth touches every aspect of my life, and it fills me with courage and hope.

I have watched you become a humbling intellect. A woman who not only has eye-opening opinions, but who can articulate them beautifully, hoping that she will imprint hearts and souls everywhere. And indeed, you have imprinted mine forever.

I have watched you become calmer and more easygoing. You spend less time worrying about others, and more time focusing on your growth and your inner peace. You extract every ounce of joy and goodness from the present. You don't allow moments to pass by without you capturing them and showing their true value and meaning. I am learning to do the same.

I have watched your interests change. You went from enjoying concerts, the outdoors, and nature (which really inspired me), to enjoying more literature, art, and writing. Every one of your writings has shown me a side of you that's made me fall more in love and that has treated me to your inner wonder. I feel fortunate.

And there is still so much more of you that I've yet to love and to experience. I haven't experienced you as my wife. The woman I will wake up beside. Who I will eat breakfast with and smile at as the sunlight spreads throughout the horizon and warms our part of the world. Who will help me make our house into a home, as she graces it with her divine femininity and her boundless splendor.

I haven't experienced you as a mother. I smile as I think about our future children, God willing. They will be so lucky to have such an intelligent, loving, thoughtful, moral, and upright woman as their mother. One who will guide them gracefully, kindly, and wonderfully through their lives.

I haven't seen you as a different professional, where you've found a profession you're truly passionate about yet. I can only imagine how much more you will grow and exceed then. How many lives you will change and how magnificent it will be.

I haven't seen your future passions yet, and just how much love, light, and awe they will elicit in me, and in others who are fortunate enough to watch you maximize them. You always make the most of things. And I'm sure then, you will do the same.

There is still so much I've yet to experience with you. What once daunted me, now fills me with hope and excitement and shows me that I needn't pay attention to my painful past. I can be grateful for this stunning present and our promising future, God willing.

And I hope that anyone who reads this feels the same. Marriage, and commitment, do not need to be painted by the brush of your past. Nor must you believe that you will fail, just because your parents, your siblings, or anyone else did in your respective communities. We're all responsible for what we choose. And we can choose to have loving, respectful relationships, where we bask in the enjoyment of seasoned love and a deepened connection.

You will doubt yourself before every major transformation. But still, you must go forward. Because success isn't built in the absence of doubt and struggle. It is built by defying them, and refusing to quit, irrespective of whatever troubles arise.

When you're looking to excel, life will require a newer you. A more refined version. One that has shed old layers and has evolved to meet the circumstances. And it will be difficult. You will be tempted to stay the same. To maintain your comfort and the routine that those around you have kept for years. A transformation will seem much too daunting.

The voices in your head will tell you that you can't do it. That if you were truly meant for something, it wouldn't be this hard. They will criticize you and dissuade you, the same way certain family members, friends, and close ones have. You will begin to doubt yourself and believe that maybe you're unfit for what you're seeking. You'll envision the difficulties, and fear will cover your veins.

But you must proceed. You can't surrender your dreams, your ambitions, and your goals because you're experiencing doubts, tribulations, and fears. Those are normal. You are meant for this journey, and you can overcome your trials. Because success has never been achieved easily. It is not found on smooth roads and clear paths. Success is built on the back of doubt. It is built as you ignore that pestering inner voice and you break the chains that your surroundings have placed upon you.

It is built when you learn to clear the debris that others have heaped upon you, so that you may find your voice, strengthen yourself, and walk forward more confidently.

Do not believe that a difficult path is indicative of your misalignment. Difficulties are there to refine you, and to push you to dispel old notions. Others will say that you can't do it, because they're stuck within their own limits. But you aren't. You're far too bold and too ambitious to trap yourself in their expectations. To lead a life of mediocrity.

Doubts and tribulations do not mean that you're on the wrong path. They are there to test you, appearing as the manifestations of all the limits others have placed upon you, that you've yet to break. And the more steps you take forward, the more they recede. The more they break. This is how you achieve your goal. How you allow your truest self to emerge through the layers others have set on you. Success will entail leaving many elements behind. Perhaps the most important one is the old beliefs you've inherited. The ones that have hindered you for far too long. You were always meant for more. You only needed to realize it, by taking the pushing through your challenges and your doubts.

Sometimes, things leave
you, because they're not
good enough for you.
Because God, and the
universe, know that you
deserve better, and that
your heart is too soft to act
on hard truths. And that
is why they act for you.

There will be moments where you will long for someone. Your heart will ache and shatter each time you recall their smile and the time you spent together. You'll wonder how the world can be so cold, and why you must be forced to endure heartbreak and to pick up the pieces when you feel you lack the strength.

Yet it's important to remember that although you may not understand the reasons now, it doesn't mean that they're nonexistent, or that you will not understand them later. You've gone through heartbreak and disappointments before. And each time, you were shown God's miracles. You saw that certain relationships and opportunities were temporary, were only meant to teach you important lessons, and were destined to fade away, so that you could continue your journey elsewhere. You wouldn't trade the wisdom and the guidance they've bestowed upon you for anything.

And this time, it will be the same. Don't allow your pain to obscure your vision or your greater sense of purpose. Because your pain is the precursor to greatness. The very impetus you need to change. God and life are not trying to smite you. They are holding your best interest, and steering you in directions that your sensitivity, your softness, and your gentleness may otherwise struggle to reach.

Life is a journey composed of varying moments. And not all are easy. Many are excruciating. But they're all necessary. For you wouldn't know happiness without sadness;

goodness without evil; and gratitude without suffering. You are being molded, not punished. You are being guided, not misdirected. You are being refined, not degraded. Just as the loving parent must redirect their child away from their potentially harmful desires, so, too, must God and the universe redirect you.

Your soft heart is a gift. But it can still go astray. And that is why calamities befall you. You need them to place you elsewhere. What you want could be your biggest downfall. It could entail you staying in the wrong relationship, and being deprived of rich growth and change. So trust that you're getting what you need. Trust that it will work out— the way it always has. That your suffering is temporary, and it's only meant to lift you beyond your old, unfitting dreams and aspirations. God, and the universe, know you're meant for more. And that is why they push the buttons that your trembling hands will not. That is why they direct you elsewhere; they see the totality of the picture, whereas your inexperienced eyes see just a part.

Because you're worth the entirety of something—the entirety of love; the entirety of respect; the entirety of joy—and not just some mere part. But you will never have it without moving forward, and without walking the journey, even while you struggle to understand it and to feel content.

Forgive them. They
never meant to hurt you.
They're struggling within
themselves, like we all are.
Let it go, and move on.
You deserve to love again.

Sometimes, people will wrong you. They will break your heart. Fail to appreciate your inner treasures and gifts. Leave you wondering, without any explanations or clarity. They will trigger your deepest wounds and leave you weeping with inconsolable sorrow. They will repay your kindness with coldness. Shut you out when you're trying to be loving and accommodating. They will be selfish while you're selfless. Choosing their needs only, as yours dwindle. They will meet your efforts with indifference, your words with silence. And you'll feel bound to these memories. Unable to progress and advance beyond the mountains of pain, so that you may reach the valleys of joy. It will be hard for you to imagine a brighter future.

Anger tethers you to the past. You relive your hurt and you color your present with it. You distrust others. You think poorly of love. You refuse to see the good in the world. Everything becomes a living, breathing memory of your old pain.

But truthfully, most people never meant to hurt you. They're battling their own traumas, difficulties, and fears, like we all are. They're stranded within themselves, wishing that it could be different. Wondering why they cannot accept love, or why gentleness and goodness terrify them. Be merciful and understanding, the same way you'd want someone to be with you.

The past repeats itself because you're still living there. Holding onto anger. Believing that somehow, if you allow the anger to burn you, then you will never experience hurt again. But that anger is not only burning you. It is setting everything around you ablaze, and warning others of danger and peril. It is suffocating you. Blinding you from moving toward new paths and endeavors. You will repeat your suffering if you continually live your life with a closed heart and with the worst assumptions.

And that's why you must learn to forgive. Not for them. But for you. For your inner peace and your freedom. For your healing. So that you do not taint your present with the past. So that you do not rob yourself of joy and keep old, pain-ridden perspectives. Let it go, so that you may free yourself and experience love again. People make mistakes because of their own traumas and challenges. But those mistakes do not need to confine you. Nor must you live your life resentfully. The world is far better than what your anguish allows you to believe. Forgiveness grants growth and freedom. The ability to realize that you're far greater than hurt and heartbreak, and that you can live fully again. Forgive them, so that you may find peace and learn to reinvent yourself to embrace the life, the love, and the gratitude you've always deserved.

It's beautiful knowing that you gave your all and you tried your best. It says a lot about you and your character. And it also allows you to walk away freely. You'll never have to wonder. You'll always know you did enough.

Y ou often predicate your worth on another's ability to see your love and to value it. You won't give your loving heart, your vibrant soul, and your determined attitude any credit if another cannot honor them and reward you with their love. You're so busy seeking external validation, that you miss your own greatness. The very qualities that restore so many people's hopes in love and in human connection.

You also fail to remember that oftentimes, another can only value you and appreciate you within the lens of their own pain and skepticism. It's not that you're worthless and your efforts are meaningless. It's that others have their own barriers to love. Barriers they often cannot see or refuse to work through.

You're different from most. You go forward, even though there's a risk of heartbreak and failure. Unlike most, you know that love is beautiful and healing. That love is transformative and holds the power to propel others beyond their biggest doubts and their deepest fears. You want to give your love, your efforts, and your openness, because you're selfless. You know that this transcends you. That the world functions on the very love and the very kindness that you so generously give.

Your character is pure and strong. You pave your own way and you love, live, and honor others openly and unconditionally—the very way it should be done. Your character is never degraded by their inability to accept you or see your worth. It stands on its own. You hold onto the value of love and the ways in which you shower others in it. So many have benefited from your ways. You aren't a follower. You won't cease your love and deprive the world of such healing, simply because others choose to be closed off and have their own impediments to it. You are a leader. Admirably deciding that you want to initiate change, and that you never want to look back and say that you wish you would have done it differently. That you should have, or could have, done more. You leave lasting impressions on everyone, because of your genuine efforts. Every one of your words, your intentions, and your goals are meaningful and genuine. Which is why they carve the souls of so many. While others lead lives of regret, you lead one of purpose and dedication.

And that's why you're admirable—but also why you often experience heartbreak. Because life must pull you away from those who cannot match what you give, until you realize your worth and decide to place your love, your efforts, and your gentle heart elsewhere.

You're not supposed to
have it all figured out.
Life is a journey, not a few
steps. Give yourself the
grace, the patience, and
the time you deserve.

You're too hard on yourself. You won't credit yourself for how far you've come. The times when your heart was shattered, and you couldn't face the world because it reminded you of an old lover. When you were insulted, mocked, and made to feel that you didn't belong because you were different. When you had close people fail to be there and show up for you.

But you'll give everyone else credit. You'll praise their journey and function as if somehow, you're less deserving. You can't seem to grasp that you're human, just like everyone else. You have a heart that beats for love, for passion, and for purpose. Eyes that see hope on the horizon, and that shed tears when you lose and you covet more. Hands that toil to lift others and to set meaning upon every path you approach. Legs that run toward those in need, no matter the cost.

You're human. And that involves being inexperienced and imperfect. You are an evolving work of art: beautiful in your own ways, yet always being added to. Always layering more colors of wisdom, openness, and experience. The true magnificence of life is being able to grow and to transcend who you once were. But you must maintain patience along the journey. Even when you're in pain, or when the road becomes difficult. When you may not understand or wish it could be different.

You're always closer than you think. These difficulties aren't present to deter you or to break you down. They're designed to strengthen you, to show you your capabilities, and to teach you the value of character and perseverance, irrespective of your emotional and physical barriers. So be unsure. Be inexperienced. Be fearful and uncertain in your journey, as you encounter failures, successes, and room for growth. You're meant to learn, not to be perfect. To add to your character. Not to regress and abandon yourself. Be patient, and trust that better days are ahead. Days so vibrant and so fulfilling, that you'll be thankful for everything you've endured.

Grieve. Let it out. Don't suppress the pain inside you. You need to express yourself, so that you don't hold onto hurt that will anchor you to the past.

Today's world often prides itself on carelessness. The ability to simply get up, toss memories out the window, and walk away as if everything is meaningless. You treat your lovingness as a weakness. A cancer you must rid your body of.

You think that by being expressive, you will be left behind. Swept away by the currents of pain and monotonous heartbreak. Moments where everyone else's recklessness seems more appealing. You curse yourself for feeling. For having rivers of emotions that course through you and push you to spill your thoughts often. It becomes easier to follow the societal trend. To turn off the faucets of emotionality and to share less about yourself. To bottle up the pain and to let it corrode your insides.

But this has never been your way. And it doesn't need to be now. Show the world your pain, your heartache, and your despair. Do not be afraid to roar when the wound is too deep. To shout when your frustrations rise. To express yourself and to seek counsel. You are not a statue, designed to sit pretty and to garner attention merely from your structure. You are a living, breathing, animated creation of the Almighty, and you were never meant to be mute, emotionless, and detached. Voice your emotional suffering. Show your heart that it has meaning, and that you deserve to express yourself.

Suppressing your pain will keep you living in the past. That's why we see so many people who wear smiles, but silently drown their inner pain by fitting into bigger crowds, and who avoid human connection and love. Our society is terrified of opening up and being the change. The individual who will proudly display their heart and their feelings, so that a greater healing can transpire.

But you don't need to succumb to their fears. You don't need to find solace in loud environments that drown your thoughts. Or in the bottom of alcoholic beverages that numb you. Set your emotions free by breathing life into them. By reminding yourself that you deserve to be seen, heard, and acknowledged, even when you're hurt and defeated.

I want to be loved for who I am. Not what I believe I need to be. And that's why I refuse to live inauthentically. To be someone I don't want to be. I'm enough as I am; I'll never think otherwise.

Growing up, love was conditional. Predicated upon the good behavior I exhibited; the grades I earned; the trouble I didn't cause; and the efficient ways I could swallow my voice, bury my needs, and refuse to be a burden. I often felt the need to be someone, or something, I wasn't. I hesitated to show my truest self—the vibrant colors of my heart representing deep emotionality and burning love; a boisterous silliness reminiscent of an unblemished soul; and eccentric interests that defied what most people enjoyed.

I didn't feel like I belonged. So, I'd morph into the version I needed to be to survive, gain acceptance, and find love. I'd plaster a smile across my face as my insides burned. Stifle my true passions as I'd pretend to like the same jokes, the same music, and the same hobbies as others. Act cruel and careless to show that I was just like the rest, and that I could follow their paths.

I wanted to fit in. It hurt to feel left out. I was always afraid that I'd be left behind—made to feel the same hurt and disappointment that I felt in my younger years. It was easier to blend in, than it was to stand out and to step into my power. A power that would radiate and often repel others, but that could eventually guide me to what I deserved—something I failed to realize then.

And nothing devastated me more than romance. My wounds would blare. Be on full display for everyone to see. I distrusted love. I couldn't believe that someone would show up for me, and love me, for who I was. I was accustomed to surviving. Being who I needed to be to maintain peace and inclusion during my childhood. I carried these patterns into adulthood thinking they'd help me progress.

Until the results were the same. My heart would break, my confidence would crumble, and I'd feel alone. I didn't understand that my inauthenticity was attracting the wrong people and leading to faulty connections.

I grew weary of attracting the wrong people. And even if things did work out, I was suffocating within the skin I was never meant to wear. I no longer desired people, places, and experiences, if it entailed me being someone I wasn't. So I started to let go. Relinquished control of the outcomes. Disassociated from others' opinions. Allowed my voice to roam free and my smile to shine amid the frowns and the critical eyes.

Still, I struggle. I often find remnants of my old self resurfacing. Feeling the need to wear labels, to like things, and to agree so that I won't be abandoned and swept away by the current of sadness. So that I won't mourn as I recede into the background, a distant sunset once luminous, but giving way to the darkness and the night's silence.

The urges to be someone or something I am not can still persist. The old wounds march to the border of my mind and demand that I shrink myself, strangle my words, and wear societal standards. But I refuse to follow them. I will continue defying them, so that I may evolve and grow stronger. I do not want to cave into the pressures. I want to be me, fully and openly, because I am proud of the man I am, and the man I aspire to become. And I refuse to be accepted for anything less.

ACKNOWLEDGMENTS

I am truly blessed to have the wonderful support that I do. I thank God, for His mercy, His guidance, and His sustenance—most important being the incredible family and friends He blessed me with.

To Hanan Chami: *Thank you, my love. You have always supported my work. You never allowed me to give up—even when my writing journey was at its lowest points. You always spotlighted my strength, my talent, and my passion. You ignited so much within me. You have shown me that love is unconditional, that I can be fully accepted for my authentic self, and that I can overcome my greatest challenges. There is no one who believes in me, loves me, and encourages me as fiercely, as passionately, and as devotedly as you. Your fun-loving spirit, your pure heart, and your gentle soul have made my life peaceful and beautiful. I love you more than you know. You are my heart; my soul; my wifey; my everything. Thank you, baby.*

To my Dad: *Thank you for always encouraging me to choose my own path and to make the most of it. I recall many of the lessons you've taught me from my early years. I carry them with me always. Thanks for showing me what it means to be genuine and true.*

To my Tata: *Thank you for being the epitome of strength. I have learned so much in watching your journey and benefited immensely from your wisdom. "Where there's a will, there's a way," you always tell me. This book, and my writing journey, attest to that.*

To Jason: *You're the best sibling a person can ask for. I love your kindness, your genuine heart, and your commitment to being who you are. You never feel the need to fit in. You're always you: a radiant, soulful human with so much light and love. You're the best. I love you more than you know.*

To my Amto Cynthia and Omo Joe: *Thank you for being second parents to me. For always treating me like I was your third son. I never felt out of place with both of you. Perhaps that's where I often found much of my strength to carry on during some pretty difficult times. Thank you.*

To my Khalto Janan: *Thank you for always supporting me and providing me with a judgment-free space to express myself and to receive your support and your love. I truly, truly appreciate you.*

To Anthony: *You're literally a brother to me. You've always encouraged me to be myself and to pursue my writing. I also gained much inspiration in watching you become a teacher—and I say the same thing: your students are truly lucky to have you. Thank you for always standing beside me.*

To Erik: *Your courage to speak the truth, to stand up for what you believe in, and to be different has always emboldened me to do the same. I have gleaned much strength from your wisdom and from your authenticity. Thank you for being like a brother to me.*

To Jaclyn: *You've supported my writing from long ago. I still recall showing you early manuscripts of my first novel. Wow. Incredible to see how far things have come. Thank you for always believing in me, encouraging me, and supporting me through some dark days.*

To Jessie: *You always believed in me, and you always pushed me to pursue what I was into. I also admire your ability to choose your own path and to not worry about what the masses think. Thank you for being you and for always being there.*

To Nadine: *Your generosity has always touched my heart. And your generosity extends far beyond society's expectation of money. It extends to promoting all of my work, always encouraging me, and always being someone I can open up to. Thank you so much.*

To Houda C: *Thank you for steering me away from anger and rage, and for always pushing me to be better. You've believed in my writing for a while. You've also never let me get down on myself. I truly appreciate you, and our friendship, more than you know.*

To Javel: *My brother. Thank you for being someone I can always open up to and be my truest self around. Your strength has fueled me deeply. With someone like you in my corner, I feel untouchable. Your words mean a lot to me.*

To Firas: *Thank you for being one of my best friends throughout the years. I admire your realness. You're never afraid to be you and to stand up for what you believe in. I can't tell you how deep of an impression that has left upon me over the years. Thank you for also supporting me.*

To Alex: *Thanks for being one of the most genuine people I know. You've always believed in my goals and were a strong voice that I often recounted when I wanted to quit. I'm blessed to have your friendship.*

To Abullah A: *My fellow creative. I still recall writing some of my best work at your house. You always inspired me with your creativity and your boldness to pursue greatness. I admire your talents, and I pray you're always successful.*

To Hassan A: *Where do I start, Khouds? You've always pushed me and wanted the best for me. You've stood beside me throughout more things than you know. I really appreciate you and your genuine heart. Thank you for everything.*

To Hassan H: *Your courage to grow and to defy so many of life's odds resonates with me. You have impacted my outlook on life and my growth beyond what you know. Thank you for supporting my work from day one.*

To Rami Y.: *Thanks for the support, the kindness, and the true friendship. I always feel like I can be open and honest around you, no matter what I'm feeling or going with. My interactions with you have shown me what I have often felt I was missing: safety. The safety to simply be me and to feel accepted. You never fail to be the great friend and blessing that reminds me of this. I also thank you and Zee for the support, and for the openness you embrace so many, including myself, with. You both have strengthened my belief in love and commitment. I appreciate you guys a lot.*

To the Writingtoinspire community: *I love you all. Thank you for supporting me, believing in me, and helping my page, and my work, grow. Without all of you, I wouldn't be here. This community has made me feel so supported and so loved. I am truly grateful and blessed.*

And to anyone else who I might have missed: *thank you for supporting me in any way that you did. Know that I am truly grateful and blessed.*

Jamal Cadoura is an author, podcaster, speaker, and life coach. He writes to inspire positive change in people's lives and express deep truths.

@writingtoinspire
The Writing to Inspire Podcast

The Stength In Our Scars
—*Bianca Sparacino*

Ceremony
—*Brianna Wiest*

Everything You'll Ever Need
(You Can Find Within Yourself)
—*Charlotte Freeman*

All That You Deserve
—*Jacqueline Whitney*

THOUGHT
CATALOG
Books

THOUGHTCATALOG.COM
NEW YORK · LOS ANGELES